D0886586

Sports Stars

LARRY BIRD

Cool Man on the Court

By Bert Rosenthal

 CHILDRENS PRESS ™

CHICAGO

Cover photograph: Howard Zryb
Inside photographs courtesy of the following:
Kevin W. Reece, pages 6, 13, 15, 16, 37, 41 and 42;
Howard Zryb, pages 8, 11 and 38;
Mary Ann Carter, pages 20, 25 and 31:
ISU photo by Howard Leistner, pages 23, 26, 33 and 34;
Don Grayston, pages 24, 29 and 44.

Library of Congress Cataloging in Publication Data

Rosenthal, Bert.
    Larry Bird, Cool Man on the Court

    (Sports stars)
    SUMMARY: Presents a biography of the National Basket-
ball Association's 1979-80 Rookie of the Year.
    1. Bird, Larry, 1956-   —Juvenile literature.
2. Basketball players—United States—Biography—Ju-
venile literature.| 1. Bird, Larry, 1956-   2. Bas-
ketball players| I. Title. II. Series.
GV884.B57R67   796.32'3'0924 | B| 80-27094
ISBN 0-516-04312-9

New 1984 Edition

    4 5 6 7 8 9 10 11 12 R 90 89 88 87 86 85 84

Sports Stars

LARRY BIRD

Cool Man on the Court

Larry Bird was the Rookie of the Year in the National Basketball Association (NBA) for the 1979-80 season. He deserved the honor. The Boston Celtics had a record of 28-53 in the 1978-79 season. Then Larry Bird joined the Celtics. They had a record of 61-21 for 1979-80. They were the best in the league.

The next year Larry surprised people. He came to the Celtics' rookie camp at Marshfield, Massachusetts. He didn't have to be there. After all, he no longer was a rookie. He was a veteran. And veteran players can report to camp later than the rookies.

The Boston Celtics won 61 games and lost 21 games in 1979-80.

But Larry Bird loves to play basketball. And so he was at camp. He went to the team's workouts. They had two a day. During the day, the Celtics practiced outside. At night, they went inside. They worked out in a high school gym.

Larry was tired and sweaty after each session. But he talked with the fans. He signed autographs. He posed for pictures. During one picture-taking session, he put his arm around the shoulders of a little child.

Larry used to be a shy country boy. That was when he entered the same rookie camp—one year earlier. Now, he was sure of himself and more friendly.

He had shown that he could play with the best in pro basketball. He had been accepted.

Bird figured on more pressure in his second season. More than in his first.

"Last year was more hectic," he said about his rookie season in the NBA. "I came into camp. I didn't have myself settled. I was new. Everybody wanted me for programs and talk shows. Now, I don't have that as much."

In his rookie year, Larry led the Celtics in scoring.

He felt he would not get as much attention. So people would expect more of him on the court.

Boston Coach Bill Fitch also was asked about the pressure on Bird. Bird in only one season had become the team's most popular player.

"I think when Larry was a kid he got a dictionary. And that word—pressure—wasn't in it," said Fitch.

Bird also said that he felt he had room for improvement in his game.

"I think everyone has weaknesses," explained Bird. He had led the Celtics in scoring average (21.3 points per game). He led in rebounding average (10.4). Both in his rookie year. "Everybody can always improve," he says.

"Some part of each player's game always needs work. If you don't shoot 100 percent, you can improve. Maybe you don't go to your right as well as your left. Maybe you force too many passes. I'm a split-second passer. I'll make turnovers [errors]. The ball might slip from my hands.

"I will try to improve on each area of my game this season. I've still got a long way to go in this league."

Larry has practiced very hard to improve his shooting.

So Larry worked to improve his shooting. He spent long hours on the court. He worked out by himself.

"I don't care how bad a shooter you are," he said. "If you practice, you'll hit. After [team] practice, I spend maybe 45 to 50 minutes alone, shooting. Everyone else has gone home. When you're real tired, that's when it helps you.

"I shot all the time when I was a little kid," he added. "That's how you do it. You just have to keep putting it up."

Gary Holland coached Bird at Springs Valley High School in Indiana. He remembers the extra work that Larry put into basketball.

"He'd come into the gym during Christmas break. He'd work out," said Holland. "He did an awful lot of running. He pushed himself with no one there to push him."

Larry Bird was born on December 7, 1956, in French Lick, Indiana. French Lick is a small town of about 2,000. It is in the southern part of the state. It actually is closer to Louisville, Kentucky, than to Indiana's biggest city, Indianapolis.

Larry had four brothers and one sister. The family never had much money.

Blond-haired Larry attended Springs Valley High. He became a basketball star. In his senior year he averaged 30.6 points. He had 20 rebounds a game. He made the All-State team.

"He definitely was the best player I ever coached," said Holland. "He was very confident. But he was conscious of his teammates. You can see that now with his unselfish play and passing. We had trouble getting him to shoot enough. Still, he shot so well. He scored a lot of points. He should have been shooting more instead of passing off."

Larry graduated from high school. He enrolled at Indiana University. The university had a big campus. It was much too large for Larry. He was just a 17-year-old from a small town. So, after about a week there, he left. He returned home.

Then Larry enrolled at Northwood Institute. Northwood is in West Baden, Indiana. It is a junior college. There were about 160 students.

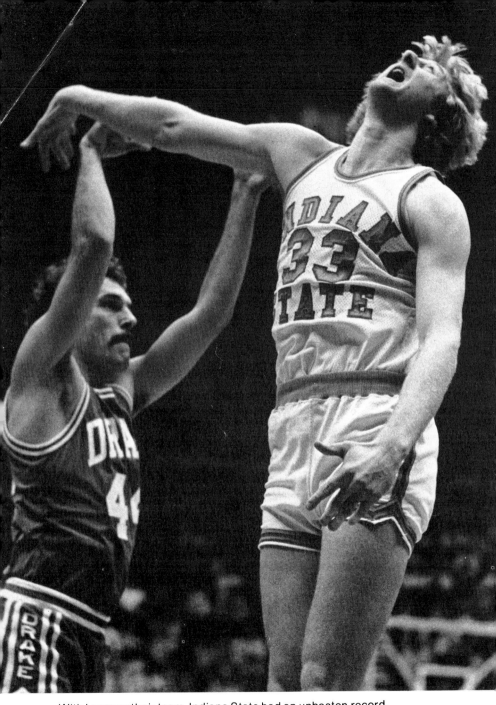

With Larry on their team, Indiana State had an unbeaten record.

This time Larry lasted two months. Then he quit again.

"He was very unsettled," said Northwood basketball coach Jack Johnson. "He had trouble attending class. He was very undisciplined."

After dropping out of Northwood, Larry took a job. He worked for the French Lick parks department. With the department, he worked at several jobs. They included driving a tractor and riding a garbage truck.

He was lured back to school in 1975 by Bob King. King was the basketball coach at Indiana State University in Terre Haute, Indiana. Larry did not play during his first year at Indiana State.

But as a sophomore Bird was a sensation. He averaged 32.8 points a game. His scoring average dipped slightly to 30.0 as a junior. But his overall game became more well-rounded. As a sophomore, he was selected as a third-team All-American. As a junior, he was chosen as a first-team All-American.

After his junior year, Larry was sure to be picked for the pros. And the Celtics used a first-round pick in the 1978 NBA draft. They took Bird. But Larry decided to stay at Indiana State. He was majoring in physical education. He wanted to get his college degree. Then he would turn pro.

Larry completed his final credits. He also completed an impressive basketball career.

For his
playing
in the
1978-79
season, Bird
was named
college
player of
the year.

Larry stayed at Indiana State until he got his college degree.

His scoring average in his senior year was 28.6, a slight drop. But he did well in rebounding, passing, and team play. Bird was named the college player of the year.

Bird led Indiana State to an unbeaten record. They ranked tops in the nation. He also guided the team to the national collegiate finals. Then Indiana State was beaten by Michigan State.

Larry wanted to win that game very badly. He wanted Indiana to win the NCAA title. He wanted to leave college on a winning note. But Michigan State won, 75-64. Bird did not play very well. His shooting was sub-par. He made more mistakes than usual.

Of course, the Michigan State defense worked on him. The Michigan State players knew they had to keep Larry in check. Then they could win the game. The plan worked.

Bird could have used an injured left thumb as an excuse. But he didn't.

Indiana State played in the national collegiate finals.

He took the loss very hard. After the game, he and his teammates went to the Indiana State rooting section. He received their cheers. He was crying. He was presented with a second-place watch. His eyes still were red.

He did not attend a post-game press conference. He stayed in the locker room for a long time. He thought about the game. Then he left quickly.

He brushed past a group of newsmen. He went up a long tunnel to the door. He slowed down only once. He signed an autograph for a fan.

Larry's team had lost the game. But Larry did not lose his fans—the many Bird-watchers.

Michigan State beat Indiana and won the NCAA title.

"I think he had a sub-par night. Yet, he played a good basketball game," said Jud Heathcote, the Michigan State coach. "Everyone seems to think the Bird is superhuman. If he doesn't score 35, they get down on him. Well, he was the leading rebounder in the game with 13. And he battled in there the whole game."

Red Auerbach is the president and general manager of the Celtics. He compared Larry to Bob Cousy. Cousy is a former star player with Boston.

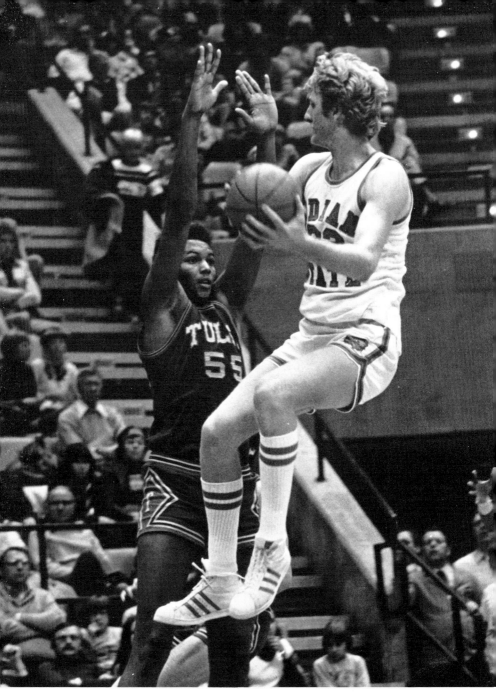

It is very hard to guard Larry Bird.

"He's a big Cousy," Auerbach said of the 6-foot-9 Bird. "I never thought I'd compare anyone with Cousy. But Larry Bird has those great hands and great vision. Everyone knows he can shoot. But other things impress me more.

"He has a great concept of the game," continued Auerbach. "He has a great feel of what's going on between the four lines [of the court]. He's got patience. He's strong and he's unselfish. And those hands and vision. Cousy was more spectacular. But that kid can do it all. He can shoot from anywhere on the court. But if he doesn't have the shot, he won't take it. He'll pass to someone open. And how he can pass. He spots the man and gives it to him. He's always anticipating on the floor. He could step into the starting lineup with any team in our league."

Of course, Auerbach hoped that Bird would be in the Celtics' starting lineup. Boston still owned the rights to him. They would keep them until the day of the 1979 NBA draft. The Celtics had to sign him by then. Or else, Bird could be drafted by another team.

Larry has an agent, Bob Woolf. They talked with the Celtics for two months. Finally, they agreed on a contract. Bird would get $650,000 a year for five years. It was the highest salary ever for an NBA rookie.

Bird started with the Celtics at the highest salary ever paid to an NBA rookie.

Bird went to a press conference announcing the signing. "I'm ready to play now," the happy Bird said. "I just wanted a fair contract. Actually, I should have told Mr. Auerbach I would have played for nothing. The money didn't have that much to do with it. I really wanted to be here [in Boston]. I'm young and have a lot to learn. I've never played on a losing team in my life. Basketball is fun for me. I don't consider it work."

During his college days, Bird did not talk much to the press. He did not like it when reporters asked about his personal life. So he avoided talking to them as much as possible.

Now, on advice from Mr. Woolf, he has loosened up. He is more open and friendly. He is relaxed. He is more sure of himself. In thinking ahead to Bird's rookie season in the NBA, Mr. Woolf said, "All I can say is you better be good."

"I'll knock 'em dead," answered Bird.

"But what if you don't?" asked Mr. Woolf.

"Then everybody will say, 'Gee, I don't know what could have happened to him. He sure was good in college.' "

They both broke up laughing.

Bird was no joke to NBA opponents. He had them crying on the inside. He had them wishing they did not have to guard him. He turned the Celtics from losers into winners. He brought a whole new group of fans to Boston Garden. And everyone enjoyed basketball again. He played the game the way it is supposed to be played. He made the Celtics think team basketball.

Because the Celtics were winning, more fans came to their games.

"Bird leads us in everything—scoring, rebounding, and passing," says Coach Fitch.

"I love basketball," said Bird. "It's fun. I like the close games. I enjoy everything about the game. I try to get every loose ball. Why not? If there's a loose ball, I'm going to dive for it."

Diving for loose balls is not often done by high-priced players. But Bird is no ordinary player. He is a cut above most other players.

"I didn't think he would be this good this season," said Mr. Auerbach. "He shoots. He rebounds. He passes. But I really like one thing about him. That's the way he goes about his business without complaining. He's the first to arrive at practice. And he's the last to leave."

"Bird leads us in everything—scoring, rebounding, and passing," said Coach Fitch. "I like what he does. He was the best rookie I've ever seen. Larry likes the game. That's what makes it so much fun. Even our practices are fun."

"If I miss a shot, that's okay," said Bird. "I know I'll do better next time. I came into the league with a good attitude. I'm confident. I always was. I worked hard all my life to play pro ball. I want to show the world and the fans I can do it. I'm sure I'll get where I want to go."

In 1984 Larry *really* helped the Celtics. They defeated the Los Angeles Lakers to win the NBA title. It was a long hard series that went to seven games. Larry was named the most valuable player of the series.

So far, Bird has not let anyone down. And no one thinks he will. He's still very young. He figures to be a pro basketball superstar for many years.

CHRONOLOGY

1956   —Larry Bird is born on December 7.

1973-74—Larry averages 30.6 points and 20 rebounds a game at Springs Valley High School in Indiana and makes the all-state team.

1974   —Bird enrolls at Indiana University, but leaves after a short time.

1974   —Bird enrolls at Northwood Institute, but stays there only two months.

1975   —Bird enrolls at Indiana State University and remains there for four years.

1976-77—As a sophomore, Larry averages 32.8 points a game.

1977-78—Larry averages 30 points a game for Indiana State and is named to the All-America team.

1978   —Bird is drafted by the Boston Celtics.

1978-79—As a college senior, his average is 28.6 points a game, and he again makes the All-America team. He also is named college player of the year.

1979   —Bird signs a five-year contract with the Celtics for $650,000 a year.

1979-80—Larry has an outstanding first season in the National Basketball Association, leading the Celtics to a 61-21 record—the best in the league. And he is named the rookie of the year.

1980-81—Larry is named a forward on the NBA All Stars first team.

1982   —Larry helps the Celtics defeat the Detroit Pistons by scoring 40 points.

1984   —Again Larry is named to the NBA All Stars first team. He is the most valuable player of the National Basketball Association championship series.